EASY PIANO

MY FIRST MOVIE THEMES SONG BOOK

A TREASURY OF FAVORITE SONGS TO PLAY

ISBN 978-1-4768-1516-9

HAL•LEONARD®
CORPORATION

7777 W. BLUEMOUND RD. P.O. BOX 13819 MILWAUKEE, WI 53213

Visit Hal Leonard Online at
www.halleonard.com

ACTION/ADVENTURE

James Bond Theme

from DR. NO

By MONTY NORMAN

MISSION: IMPOSSIBLE
THEME

from the Paramount Motion Picture MISSION: IMPOSSIBLE

By LALO SCHIFRIN

RAIDERS MARCH

from the Paramount Motion Picture
RAIDERS OF THE LOST ARK

Music by JOHN WILLIAMS

ANIMATION

HALLELUJAH

featured in the DreamWorks Motion Picture SHREK

Words and Music by
LEONARD COHEN

Moderately slow, in 2

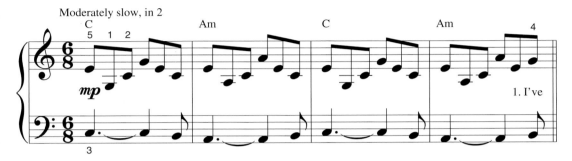

1. I've

heard there was a se-cret chord __ that Da-vid played, __ and it
2.-5. *(See additional lyrics)*

pleased the Lord, __ but you don't _____ real-ly care for mu-sic, __

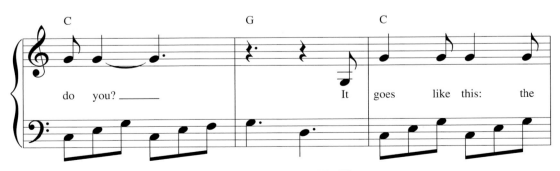

do you? _____ It goes like this: the

Additional Lyrics

2. Your faith was strong, but you needed proof.
   You saw her bathing on the roof.
   Her beauty and the moonlight overthrew you.
   She tied you to a kitchen chair.
   She broke your throne; she cut your hair.
   And from your lips she drew the Hallelujah.
   Chorus

3. Maybe I have been here before.
   I know this room; I've walked this floor.
   I used to live alone before I knew you.
   I've seen your flag on the marble arch.
   Love is not a victory march.
   It's a cold and it's a broken Hallelujah.
   Chorus

4. There was a time you let me know
   What's real and going on below.
   But now you never show it to me, do you?
   And remember when I moved in you,
   The holy dark was movin' too,
   And every breath we drew was Hallelujah.
   Chorus

5. Maybe there's a God above,
   And all I ever learned from love
   Was how to shoot at someone who outdrew you.
   And it's not a cry you can hear at night.
   It's not somebody who's seen the light.
   It's a cold and it's a broken Hallelujah.
   Chorus

If We Hold On Together

from THE LAND BEFORE TIME

Words and Music by JAMES HORNER
and WILL JENNINGS

Smoothly

With pedal

Don't lose your way with each pass-ing day. You've come so far, don't throw it a-way.
Souls in the wind must learn how to bend, seek out a star, hold on to the end.

Live be-liev-ing dreams are for weav-ing, won-ders are wait-ing to
Val - ley, moun-tain, there is a foun-tain wash-es our tears all a-

You've Got a Friend in Me

from Walt Disney's TOY STORY

Music and Lyrics by
RANDY NEWMAN

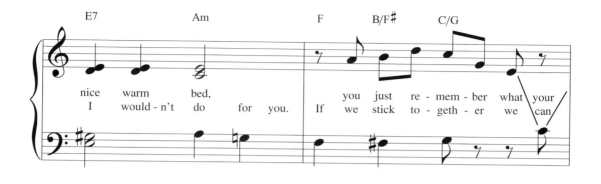

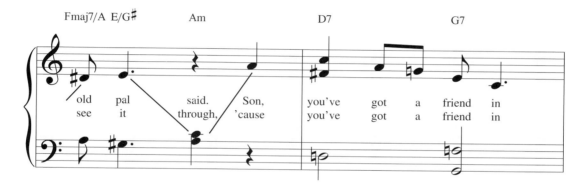

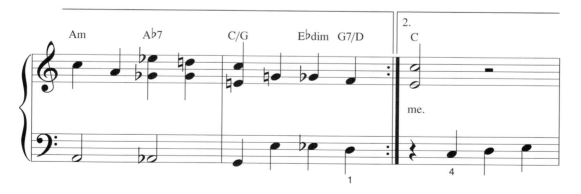

COMEDY

THE PINK PANTHER

from THE PINK PANTHER

By HENRY MANCINI

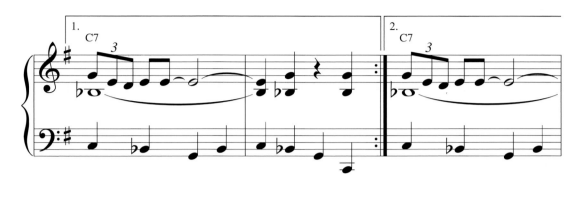

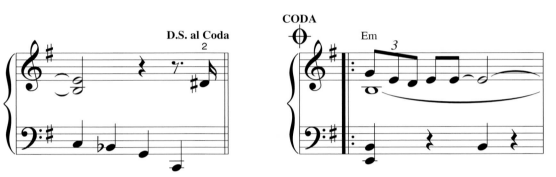

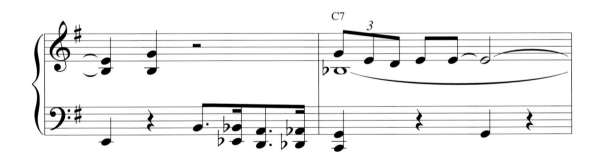

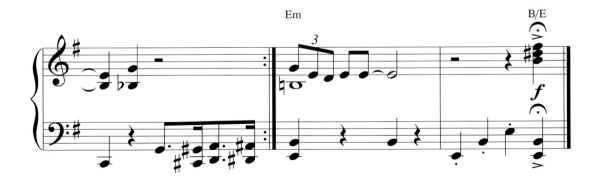

Sisters

from the Motion Picture Irving Berlin's WHITE CHRISTMAS

Words and Music by
IRVING BERLIN

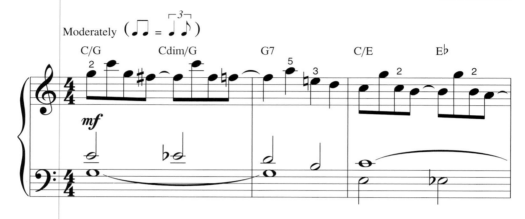

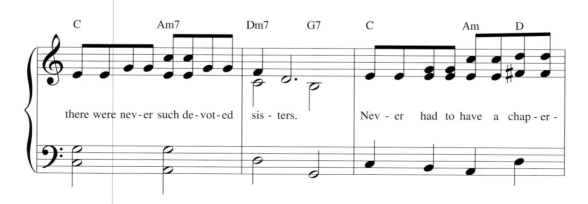

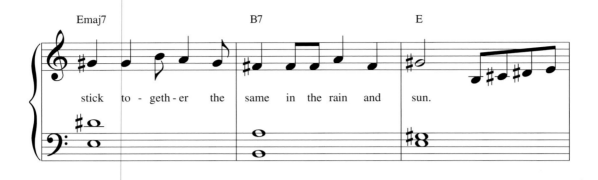

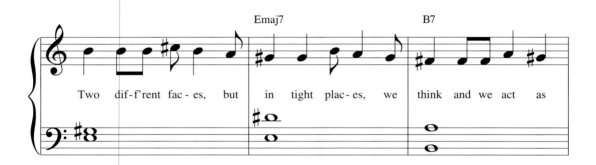

SOUL BOSSA NOVA

from AUSTIN POWERS: INTERNATIONAL MAN OF MYSTERY

Music by QUINCY JONES

EPIC DRAMAS

Somewhere, My Love

Lara's Theme from
DOCTOR ZHIVAGO

Lyric by PAUL FRANCIS WEBSTER
Music by MAURICE JARRE

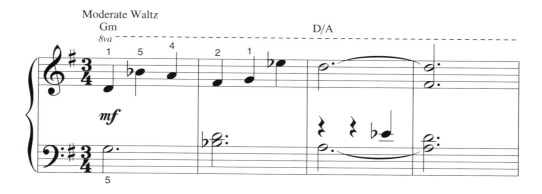

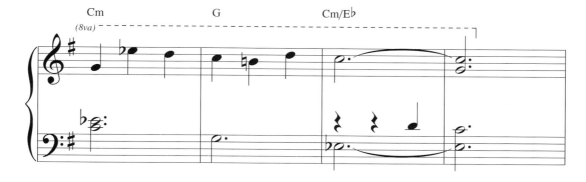

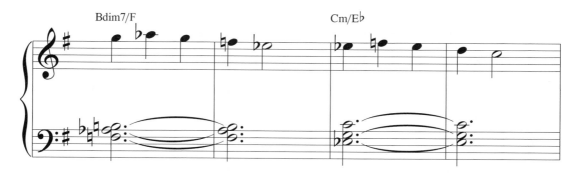

41

day, _____ when - ev - er the

F   B♭   D7

spring   breaks   through. _____

G

You'll   come   to   me _____
Till   then,   my   sweet, _____

G/B   B♭dim   Am7

_____   out   of   the   long   a - go, _____
_____   think   of   me   now   and   then. _____

GABRIEL'S OBOE

from the Motion Picture THE MISSION

Words and Music by
ENNIO MORRICONE

My Heart Will Go On

(Love Theme from 'Titanic')

from the Paramount and Twentieth Century Fox Motion Picture TITANIC

Music by JAMES HORNER
Lyric by WILL JENNINGS

Moderately

mp

With pedal

Ev - 'ry night in my dreams I see you, I feel you, that is how I know you go on. ___

Far a-cross the dis-tance and spac-es be-

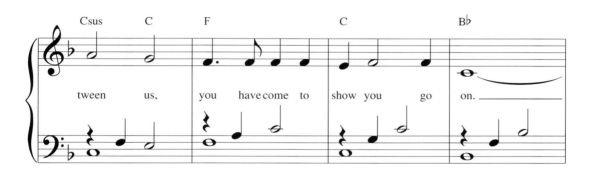

tween us, you have come to show you go on.

Near, far, wher-ev - er you are,

I be-lieve that the heart does go on.

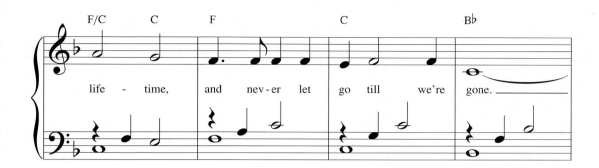

life - time, and nev-er let go till we're gone. ____

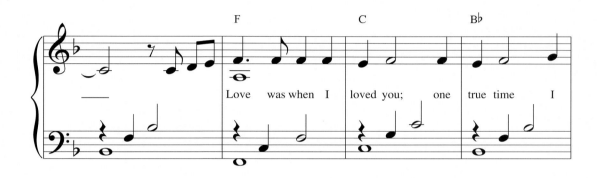

____ Love was when I loved you; one true time I

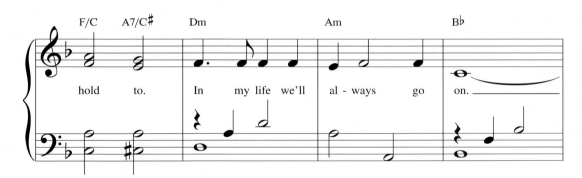

hold to. In my life we'll al - ways go on. ____

D.S. al Coda

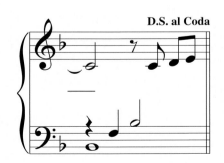

____

CODA

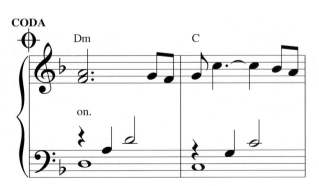

on.

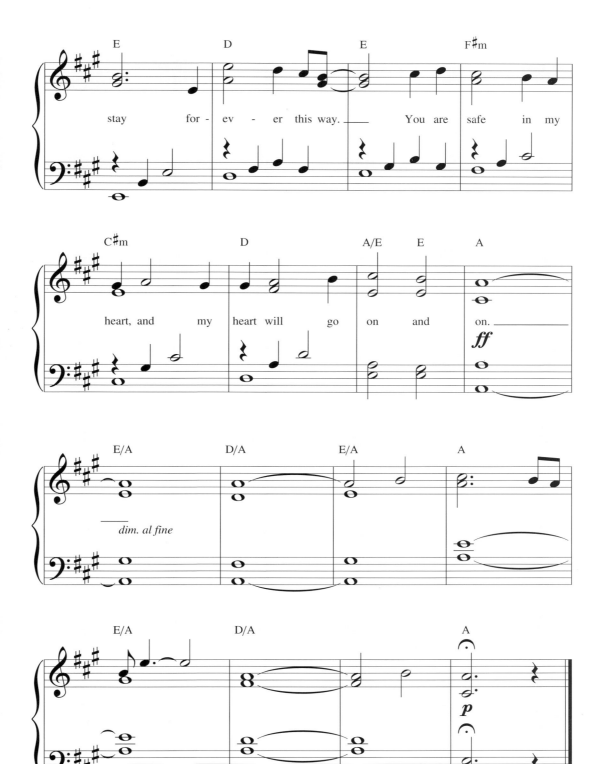

FANTASY

STAR TREK®
THE MOTION PICTURE

Theme from the Paramount Picture
STAR TREK: THE MOTION PICTURE

By JERRY GOLDSMITH

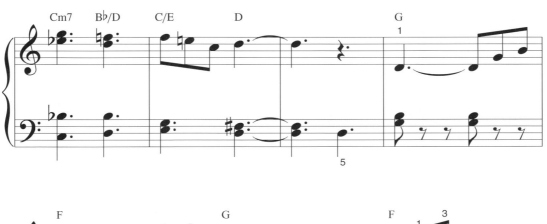

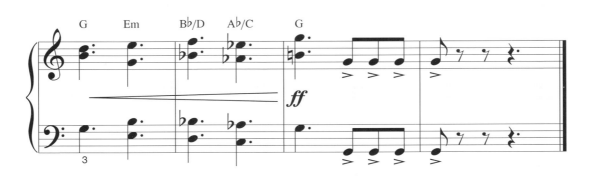

A NARNIA LULLABY

from Walt Disney Pictures' and Walden Media's
THE CHRONICLES OF NARNIA:
THE LION, THE WITCH AND THE WARDROBE

Music by HARRY GREGSON-WILLIAMS

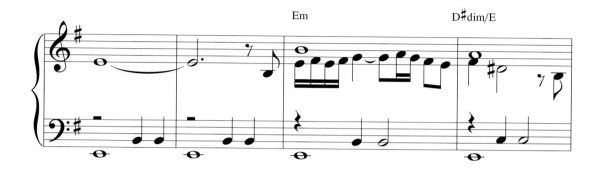

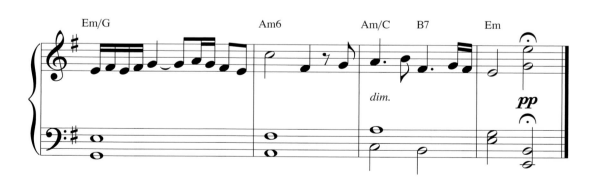

STAR WARS
(MAIN THEME)

from the Lucasfilm Ltd. Production STAR WARS,
THE EMPIRE STRIKES BACK, and RETURN OF THE JEDI –
Twentieth Century Fox Releases

By JOHN WILLIAMS

MOVIE MUSICALS

Over *the* Rainbow

from THE WIZARD OF OZ

Music by HAROLD ARLEN
Lyric by E.Y. "YIP" HARBURG

New York, New York

from ON THE TOWN

Lyrics by BETTY COMDEN
and ADOLPH GREEN
Music by LEONARD BERNSTEIN

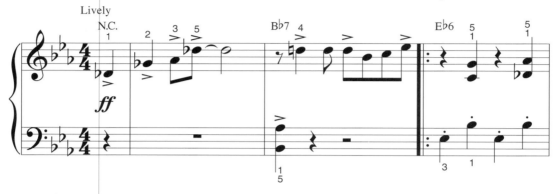

We've got ___ one day ___
The fa - mous plac -
Man - hat - tan wom -

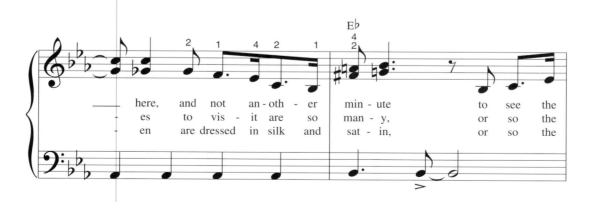

here, and not an - oth - er min - ute to see the
es to vis - it are so man - y, or so the
en are dressed in silk and sat - in, or so the

York, New York, _____

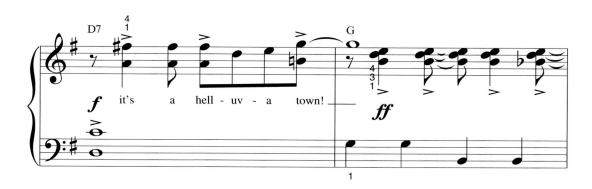

f it's a hell - uv - a town! _____ *ff*

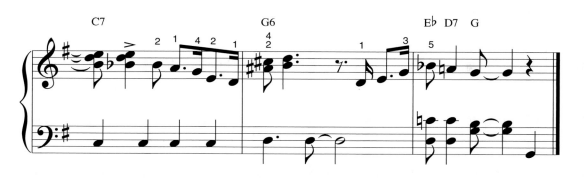

Singin' in the Rain

from SINGIN' IN THE RAIN

Lyric by ARTHUR FREED
Music by NACIO HERB BROWN

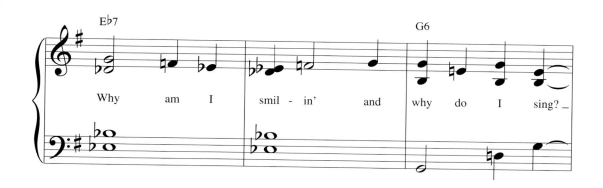

Why am I smil - in' and why do I sing? —

— Why does De - cem - ber seem

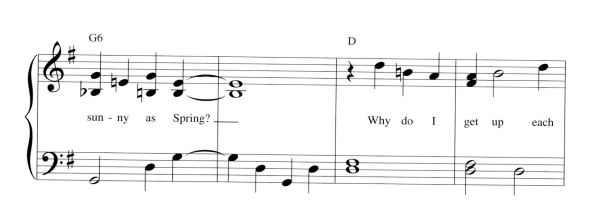

sun - ny as Spring? — Why do I get up each

morn - ing to start — hap - py and

ROMANCE

As Time Goes By

from CASABLANCA

Words and Music by
HERMAN HUPFELD

Falling Slowly

from the Motion Picture ONCE

Words and Music by GLEN HANSARD
and MARKETA IRGLOVA

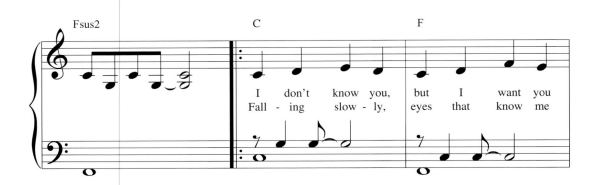

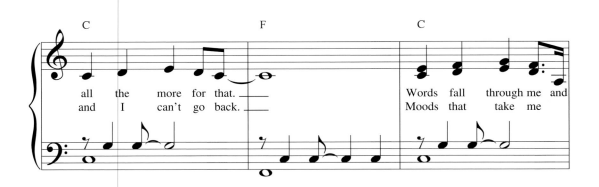

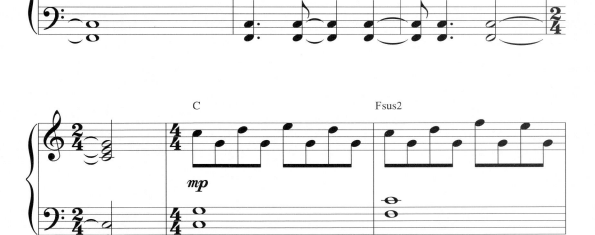

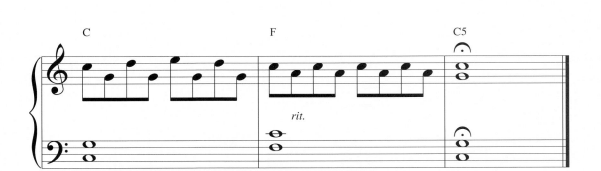

Somewhere in Time

from SOMEWHERE IN TIME

Words by B.A. ROBERTSON
Music by JOHN BARRY

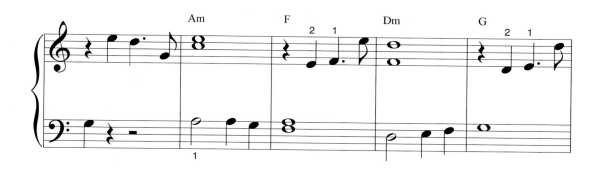

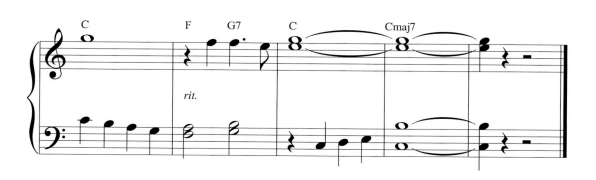

SPORTS

Hands of Time

Theme from the Screen Gems Television Production
BRIAN'S SONG

Words by ALAN BERGMAN and MARILYN BERGMAN
Music by MICHEL LEGRAND

CHARIOTS *of* FIRE

from CHARIOTS OF FIRE

By VANGELIS

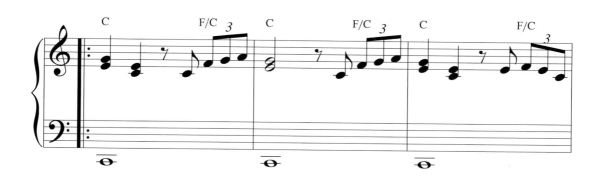

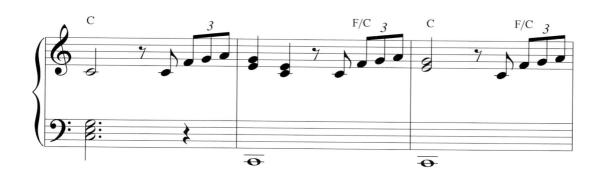

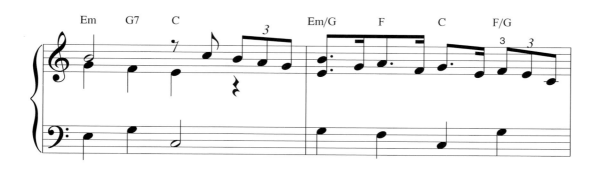

WE ARE THE CHAMPIONS

featured in THE MIGHTY DUCKS

Words and Music by
FREDDIE MERCURY

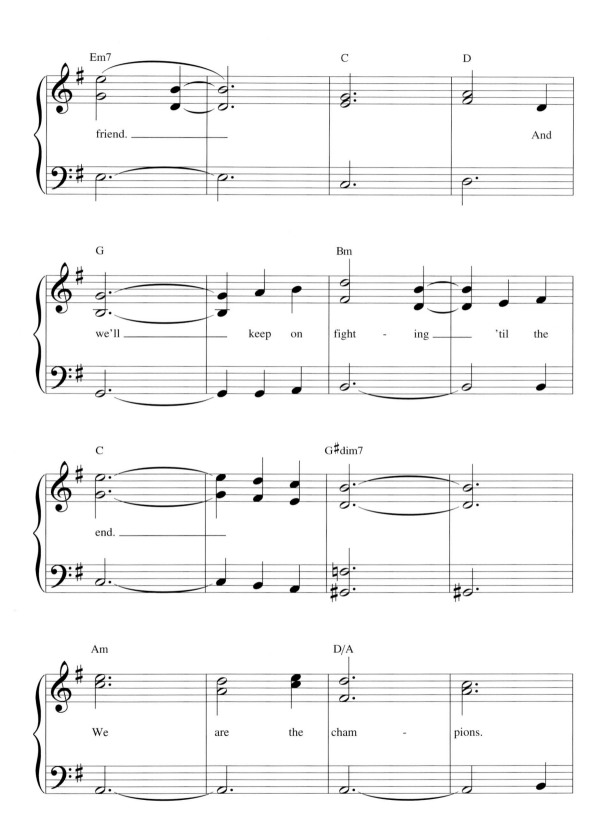

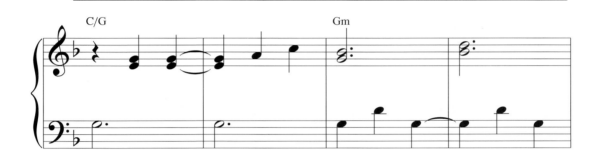

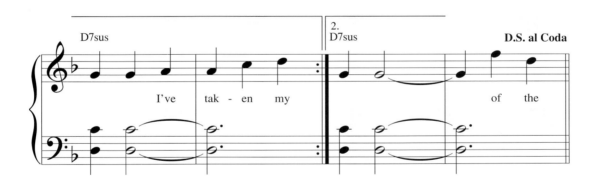

I've tak - en my

of the

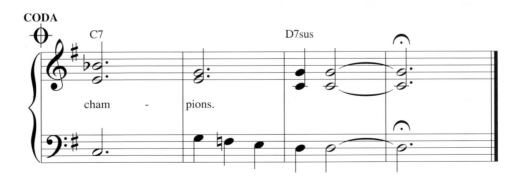

cham - pions.

WESTERNS

HOW THE WEST WAS WON
{ MAIN TITLE }

from
HOW THE WEST WAS WON

Lyrics by KEN DARBY
Music by ALFRED NEWMAN

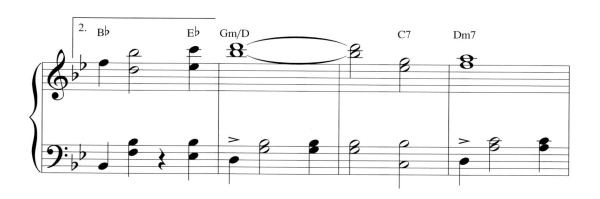

THE MAGNIFICENT SEVEN

from THE MAGNIFICENT SEVEN

By ELMER BERNSTEIN

Jessica's Theme
(Breaking In the Colt)

from THE MAN FROM SNOWY RIVER

By BRUCE ROWLAND

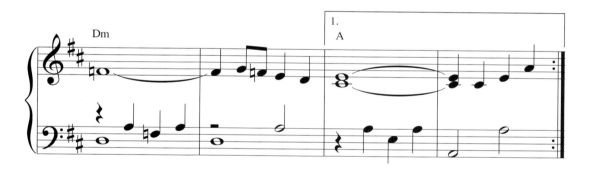

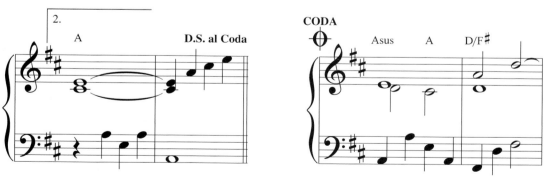

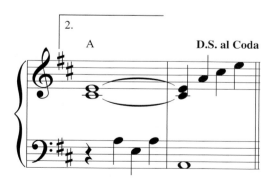